This book is for: _____

From: _____

On: _____

Let every whisper and every shout bring you closer to God!

FRIENDS WITH GOD

DISCOVER
HOW TO PRAY

Written by Jeff White
Illustrated by David Harrington

Group | **lifetree**

Visit **MyLifetree.com** for more fun, faith-building stuff for kids!

Friends With God Discover How to Pray

Copyright © 2019 Group Publishing, Inc./0000 0001 0362 4853
Lifetree™ is an imprint of Group Publishing, Inc.

Visit our website: **group.com**

Credits
Author: Jeff White
Illustrator: David Harrington
Chief Creative Officer: Joani Schultz
Senior Editors: Jan Kershner and Candace McMahan
Assistant Editor: Cherie Shifflett
Cover Design: Stephen Caine
Interior Design: Darrin Stoll

Scripture quotations are taken from the Holy Bible, New Living Translation, copyright © 1996, 2004, 2007, 2013, 2015 by Tyndale House Foundation. Used by permission of Tyndale House Publishers, Inc., Carol Stream, Illinois 60188. All rights reserved.

ISBN 978-1-4707-5502-7 (hardcover)
ISBN 978-1-4707-5505-8 (ePub)

10 9 8 7 6 5 4 3 2 1   28 27 26 25 24 23 22 21 20 19

Printed in China.
001 China 1018

TABLE OF CONTENTS

LET'S TALK WITH GOD!

God loves you *so much* and wants you to be his friend. And friends talk to each other. That's what prayer is—talking to God, your friend.

This book will show you what prayer is and how you can do it. Prayer can be fun, and you'll discover lots of great ways to tell God how you feel and what you're thinking about.

So join me and other friends of God to discover how prayer can make you happier, smarter, and kinder. It's going to be fun!

Your friend,
Jesus

PRAYER IS SIMPLY TALKING TO GOD

*"I am praying to you because
I know you will answer, O God.
Bend down and listen as I pray."*

Psalm 17:6

ADAM

When I was in the Garden of Eden, all my neighbors were animals. They came in all shapes, colors, and sizes, and I gave every one of them a name. But as beautiful as all those creatures were, I couldn't really talk to them. They didn't talk back, and I was pretty sure they didn't understand a word I said. (Except maybe the dog. The dog seemed to know the word *treat* really well!)

But there was one person I could talk to: God. God listened. God cared. God even talked back. I was the very first person to pray to God, since I was also the first person to talk with God. And after God made Eve, my wife, I found that talking with God and Eve were just about the same thing.

Praying isn't hard. All you have to do is talk to God. You already know how to talk with your friends, parents, teachers, brothers and sisters, and other people in your life. Easy, right? Well, prayer is talking, too. You're simply talking to God instead of people.

Let's Pray

Talk to God about what you're going to do today.

Here's an example of what it's like to talk to God:

"God, today I'm taking a test at school, and I'm not very excited about it. But I am looking forward to seeing my friends again. Amen."

 Write your own prayer here.

You just talked to God! Wasn't that easy?
Let's do it again soon!

GOD WANTS YOU TO PRAY

"When you pray, I will listen."

Jeremiah 29:12

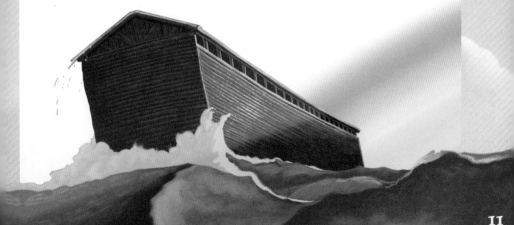

NOAH

God loved making the world and all the people in it. But after a while, many of those people stopped caring about God. They wanted to do their own thing and ignore God. They didn't listen to him.

But not me. I listened to God. I loved talking with him, and he loved talking with me. That's why God gave my family and me a second chance. When God sent a huge flood to destroy everything in the world, he saved my family and me on a huge boat.

When you pray, you invite God into your life. So when the floods of life come your way, God is always there to help you through them.

 # Let's Pray

Tell God about one thing that overwhelms you, something that feels too big for you to handle by yourself.

Here's an example of what you can say to God today:

"God, I'm so glad that you're bigger than my math problems. That makes me happy, and I love you for that."

 Write your own prayer here.

Sweet! God loves hearing from you!

You can Pray Anytime

"Pray in the Spirit at all times and on every occasion. Stay alert and be persistent in your prayers for all believers everywhere."

Ephesians 6:18

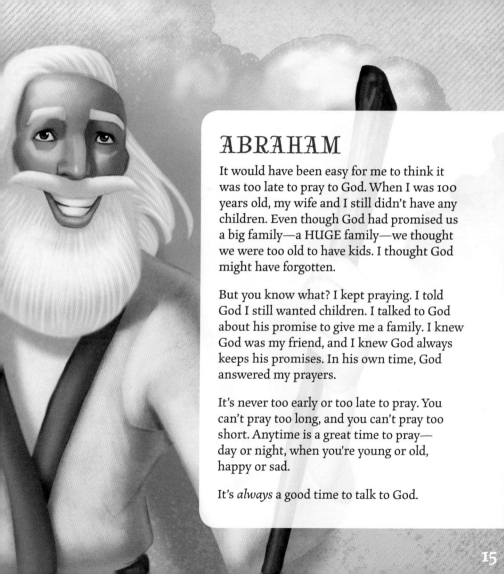

ABRAHAM

It would have been easy for me to think it was too late to pray to God. When I was 100 years old, my wife and I still didn't have any children. Even though God had promised us a big family—a HUGE family—we thought we were too old to have kids. I thought God might have forgotten.

But you know what? I kept praying. I told God I still wanted children. I talked to God about his promise to give me a family. I knew God was my friend, and I knew God always keeps his promises. In his own time, God answered my prayers.

It's never too early or too late to pray. You can't pray too long, and you can't pray too short. Anytime is a great time to pray— day or night, when you're young or old, happy or sad.

It's *always* a good time to talk to God.

15

Let's Pray

 Write your prayer here.

Take a moment, right now, to pray to God. Maybe you can tell God about your day.

Here's an example of what you might say to God today:

"God, today I played outside with my friends, and I had a lot of fun. Even though I didn't talk to you then, I knew you were with me. I'm glad I can talk to you anytime. Amen."

Great job! Don't forget— you can pray anytime, day or night.

YOU CAN PRAY ANYWHERE

"In every place of worship...pray with holy hands lifted up to God."

1 Timothy 2:8

JOSEPH

Ever since I was a kid, I've always been on the move. I was thrown down a hole, I was sold as a slave, I traveled to a foreign country, I was tossed in a prison, and I even served alongside a king. And everywhere I went, I talked to God.

No matter where we are, God is always there. And God is always ready to listen to our prayers.

You can talk to God inside, outside, and upside down. You can pray at home, at church, at school, or at a restaurant. You can talk to God whether you're alone or with other people. God will listen to you anywhere you are.

Let's Pray

Find a spot you've never prayed before.
Take a moment to tell God how you're feeling today.

> Try praying in your backyard,
> in your family's car, or in a store.

 Write your prayer here.

Wasn't that cool?
You can pray anywhere you want.

You Can Pray About Anything

"*The earnest prayer of a righteous person has great power and produces wonderful results.*"

James 5:16

MIRIAM

When my baby brother Moses was born, I was scared for him. Pharaoh wanted all the young Hebrew boys to be killed, and since my brother was a Hebrew, I thought he was doomed.

I could have complained to God. I could have told God I was mad. I could have cried to God and said I didn't think it was fair. And you know what? God would have listened to me, no matter what.

But instead, I told God I was going to do something. I followed my brother and kept a close eye on him. And when the Egyptian princess found Moses in a basket in the river, I made sure he was taken care of. God answered my prayer and saved Moses!

God will listen to any of your prayers, no matter how you feel or what you say. If you're mad or scared, like I was, you can ask God to help you be brave. God can always help you, no matter what you ask him.

Let's Pray

 Write your prayer here.

What's one big, hard question you'd like to ask God? God's not afraid of our questions. Go ahead and ask him. Then watch to see how God answers.

Here's an example:

"Dear God, today I'm not feeling very happy. I'm kind of worried, and I don't know what to do. Please help me. Amen."

It feels so good to tell God how we're feeling. God always cares.

You Can Pray Even When You Don't Know What to Say

"And the Holy Spirit helps us in our weakness. For example, we don't know what God wants us to pray for. But the Holy Spirit prays for us with groanings that cannot be expressed in words."

Romans 8:26

MOSES

When God told me to ask Pharaoh to set the Israelites free from slavery, I was nervous. I wasn't the kind of person who liked to speak up. I wasn't great with words or making speeches. I didn't even know what I would say!

I bet you're a lot like me sometimes. You probably have moments when you're not sure what to say, whether it's with your friends, your parents, or even with God. But God knows your heart, even when you fumble over the words. God will listen anyway—he can hear your words *and* your heart.

Let's Pray

Your best friend is probably the easiest person to talk to. Right now, tell God something you'd tell your best friend.

Here's an example:

"God, I'm trying to decide if I should go to the park with my friends or help my mom with the laundry. What do you think?"

 Write your prayer here.

God is listening to you, just like a real friend does. Because he IS a real friend! So keep talking!

Your Prayers Can Be Short

"When you pray, don't babble on and on as the Gentiles do. They think their prayers are answered merely by repeating their words again and again."

Matthew 6:7

AARON

I was having a hard time being the leader of the Israelites. We were lost in the desert, Moses had been gone a long time up on the mountain, and the people were getting restless. They wanted a new god to worship, and they wanted it now!

I panicked. I didn't know what to do, so I gave in to their wishes. But there's one thing I could have done instead, and it would have been the easiest thing in the world. I could have looked to God and said "Help!"

That would have been a short prayer for sure. Just one word! But God would have heard me and helped me. Instead, I ignored God and tried to solve the problem myself, and that turned into a disaster.

When you want to talk to God, you don't always have to go on and on and on. God doesn't need a long explanation—he knows your heart. Even when your prayers are short, God hears you.

Let's Pray

Pray a one-sentence or even a one-word
prayer about anything you want.

Here's an example:

"Dear God, today has been a great day!"

 Write your prayer here.

*Super! Prayers don't have to be long.
Every little word counts.*

God Always Listens to Your Prayers

"And we are confident that he hears us whenever we ask for anything that pleases him."

1 John 5:14

29

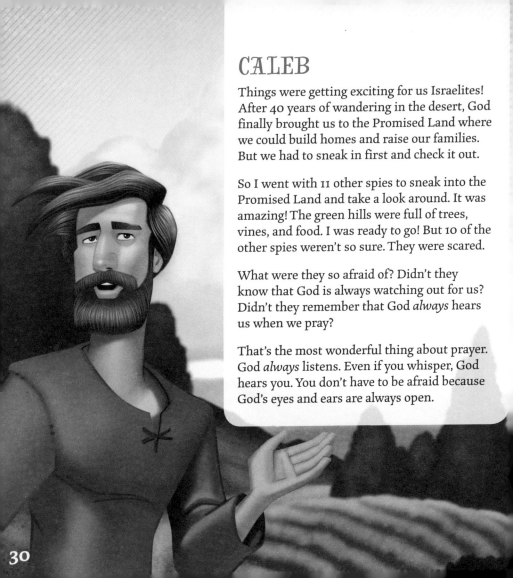

CALEB

Things were getting exciting for us Israelites! After 40 years of wandering in the desert, God finally brought us to the Promised Land where we could build homes and raise our families. But we had to sneak in first and check it out.

So I went with 11 other spies to sneak into the Promised Land and take a look around. It was amazing! The green hills were full of trees, vines, and food. I was ready to go! But 10 of the other spies weren't so sure. They were scared.

What were they so afraid of? Didn't they know that God is always watching out for us? Didn't they remember that God *always* hears us when we pray?

That's the most wonderful thing about prayer. God *always* listens. Even if you whisper, God hears you. You don't have to be afraid because God's eyes and ears are always open.

Let's Pray

Thank God for listening to your prayers.

Here's an example:

"Dear God, thank you for hearing me, even when I don't say my words out loud. Amen."

God just heard your prayer! And God hears you every time you pray.

✏️ **Write your prayer here.**

Whenever You're Worried, Pray Instead

"Don't worry about anything; instead, pray about everything. Tell God what you need, and thank him for all he has done."

Philippians 4:6

RAHAB

I was worried. Two Israelite spies had come to Jericho to check things out. They said God was going to help their people conquer Jericho, so I decided to help them. I kept them safe and helped them escape.

But I was worried! I'd heard lots of stories about how God had helped the Israelites conquer other cities. Even though Jericho had a mighty wall to protect us, I knew that God was way bigger than our wall.

So I decided to put my trust in God instead of worrying. Those two spies said God would protect me and my family. I didn't need to get upset. Instead, I needed to pray. I was thankful that God would keep me safe.

 Write your prayer here.

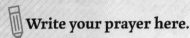

Tell God about something that worries you.

Here's an example:

"God, I can't stop thinking about that mean kid at school. I'm always worried about what he'll do next. Help me not to worry anymore. Amen."

Don't you feel better? It always helps to let God carry your worries.

34

You can Sing Your Prayers

"Be filled with the Holy Spirit, singing psalms and hymns and spiritual songs among yourselves, and making music to the Lord in your hearts."

Ephesians 5:18-19

DAVID

I talked to God a *lot*. As a young shepherd in the fields and later, as the king of Israel, I prayed all the time, about everything.

Sometimes I even sang my prayers! A lot of the psalms you read in the Bible were actually songs I wrote as prayers to God. I could sing my prayers to God, by myself or with my friends. God heard every word and every note...and he loved it.

You can sing your prayers, too. Sometimes people have an easier time singing instead of talking. You can make up your own songs, or you can sing along to one of your favorite praise songs. Either way, it's music to God's ears!

Let's Sing!

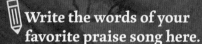

Sing a prayer to God.

What's one of your favorite praise songs? Sing or hum it aloud as a prayer to God.

You have a wonderful voice! And you just made God smile!

Write the words of your favorite praise song here.

You can Write Your Prayers

"Kind words are like honey—sweet to the soul and healthy for the body."

Proverbs 16:24

DAVID

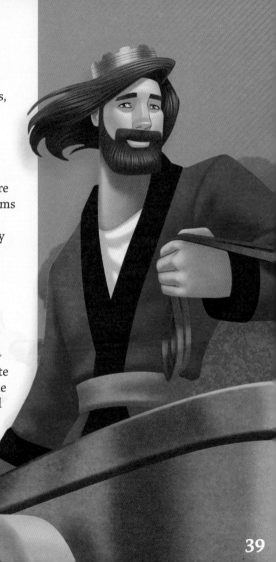

I've been through a lot of crazy stuff in my life. There have been ups and downs, happy times and sad times, wins and losses, good days and bad days. But through every single moment, I could talk to God about what was going on.

I even wrote down a lot of prayers. There are 75 of my prayers in the book of Psalms in the Bible. Yep, those psalms—some are songs, and some are poems—are my prayers to God.

Writing them down was a great way for me to tell God how I felt. And later I loved to read those prayers and even pray them again. I'll never forget those prayers because I wrote them down.

You can write prayers, too! You can write them as poems, or you can just write the same words you'd say to God if you said them out loud. Give it a try today!

Let's Pray

Write a short poem to God here on this page.

Here's an example:

Every night and every day, God will hear me when I pray.
When I work and when I play, God will guide me all the way.

 Write your prayer here.

You did the "write" thing! God loves all our prayers.

You Can Pray About The Same Thing Again and Again

"Keep on asking, and you will receive what you ask for. Keep on seeking, and you will find. Keep on knocking, and the door will be opened to you."

Matthew 7:7

HANNAH

The one thing I wanted more than anything was a baby. I prayed and prayed and prayed and prayed for God to give me one. I begged. I cried. I shouted. I whispered. I prayed out loud. I prayed in my head.

And you know what? God heard me every time.

It took a few years, but God answered my prayers with a "yes." It was worth the wait! God gave me a precious little boy, and I named him Samuel. I was so grateful! When my son was just a few years old, I dedicated him to God.

God always hears you, even when it seems you're not getting an answer for a long, long time. So keep on praying! You can talk to God about the same thing again and again. God is listening!

Let's Pray

For a whole week, talk to God every day about something that's important to you. Ask God to guide you as you do it.

Here's an example:

"God, I've been praying about this every day, and I want to tell you about it again. Please be with my friend who's having a hard time right now. She's still sad, and I want her to feel better. Amen."

 Write your prayer here.

You did it! No matter how many times you say it, God hears you every time.

You can Draw your Prayers

"I have filled him with the Spirit of God, giving him great wisdom, ability, and expertise in all kinds of crafts."

Exodus 31:3

BEZALEL

I'm an artist. You probably don't hear a lot of stories about me. But I was given a very, *very* important job. God filled me with his Spirit so I could create beautiful art for him in his Temple.

I designed all kinds of things—the Ark of the Covenant, furniture, tapestries, the priests' robes, jewelry, lamps, even the Temple itself! I loved creating art for God!

Art and creativity are great ways to show God what you're thinking and feeling. You can honor God through your art.

You can even pray to God through your art. Sometimes, when you're not sure of the words you want to say, you can draw God a picture that shows him what you're feeling. And God understands exactly what you're trying to tell him.

Let's Draw

Draw your picture here.

Draw God a picture of one thing you're thankful for.

Here's an example:

Maybe you can draw a picture of your pet to show God how thankful you are for your animal friend.

You're an amazing artist! If God had a fridge, your picture would be hanging there right now.

You Can Ask God to Help You

"Never stop praying."

1 Thessalonians 5:17

GIDEON

We had a *big* problem. The Midianites were making our lives miserable. They ruined our crops and stole our animals. We were running out of food to eat! We needed to do something, but the Midianites were way too strong and powerful.

I was the last person you'd think could help. I was young and afraid. But God had chosen *me* to lead my people to victory. One small problem: I had no idea how to do it. But there was one thing I could do. I could ask God for help—and I did.

That's all it took. God heard me and told me what to do. We beat the Midianite army with a few horns, some torches, and a whole lot of God's power.

When you pray, you can ask God to help you. It doesn't matter how big or small your problem is, God is ready to help. Just ask!

Let's Pray

Ask God to help you with a problem you're facing.

Here's an example:

"Dear God, I can't seem to figure out how to get along with my friend at school. Can you show me something I can do to make it better? Amen."

There you go! God's bigger than any problem you have.

 Write your prayer here.

YOU CAN TELL GOD HOW YOU'RE FEELING, NO MATTER WHAT YOU'RE FEELING

"When doubts filled my mind, your comfort gave me renewed hope and cheer."

Psalm 94:19

ABIGAIL

My husband was not a very nice man. He was mean and nasty to just about everyone, even people who were trying to help him.

I didn't know how to make him be nice! He was putting our lives in danger with his bad temper.

I felt terrible and helpless. So I told God exactly how I was feeling. And sure enough, God helped me find a way to keep us safe.

God will listen to anything you have to say. You can tell God how you're feeling, especially when you feel frightened and helpless. The first—and best—thing to do when you're scared is ask God for help. When you pray, don't be afraid to tell God what's on your heart and mind.

Let's Pray

Tell God about something that's really bugging you.

Here's an example:

"God, every time my little sister hits me, I'm the one who gets in trouble. What can I do to get her to stop bothering me so much? Amen."

 Write your prayer here.

Well done. Don't forget, you can tell God anything.

x

You Can Ask God for Joy

"I pray that God, the source of hope, will fill you completely with joy and peace because you trust in him."

Romans 15:13

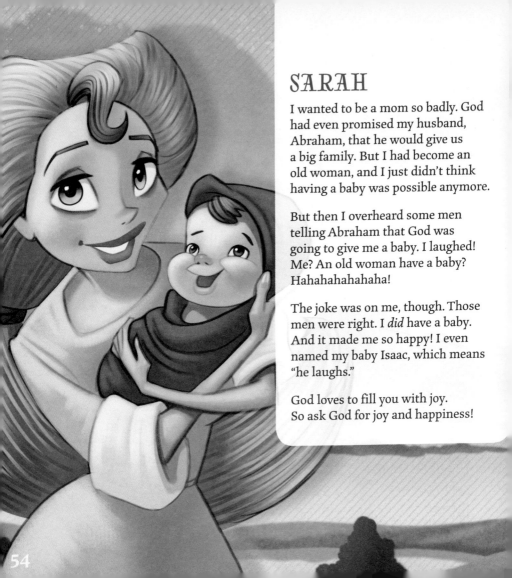

SARAH

I wanted to be a mom so badly. God had even promised my husband, Abraham, that he would give us a big family. But I had become an old woman, and I just didn't think having a baby was possible anymore.

But then I overheard some men telling Abraham that God was going to give me a baby. I laughed! Me? An old woman have a baby? Hahahahahahaha!

The joke was on me, though. Those men were right. I *did* have a baby. And it made me so happy! I even named my baby Isaac, which means "he laughs."

God loves to fill you with joy. So ask God for joy and happiness!

Let's Pray

Ask God to help you be joyful today.

Here's an example:

"Dear God, I really could use an extra smile today. Please help me be joyful! Amen."

Yahoo! Let the joy start now!

 Write your prayer here.

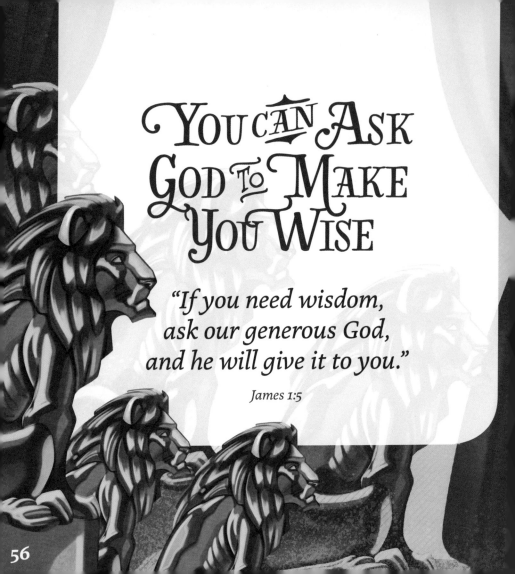

You can Ask God to Make You Wise

*"If you need wisdom,
ask our generous God,
and he will give it to you."*

James 1:5

56

SOLOMON

If God told you that you could have anything you wanted, what would you ask him for?

I got to do exactly that! And you know what I asked God for? Wisdom.

That made God very, very happy. In fact, God was so pleased that he gave me wisdom—and lots more. I was able to make smart decisions and understand things that other people didn't understand.

There are lots of ways to ask God for wisdom. You can say, "God, please give me wisdom." Or "God, help me see things the way you see them." Or "God, help me understand."

God wants to help you be wise. Just ask him.

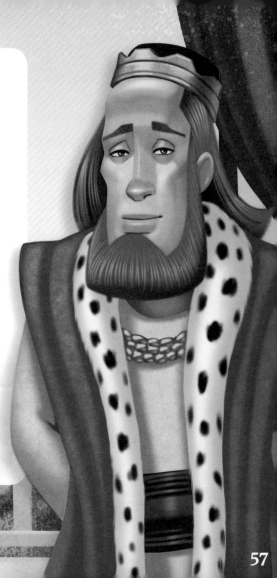

Let's Pray

Ask God to help you be wise about a situation in your life.

Here's an example:

"God, I'm not sure how to be wise about what's going on at school, but I'd love it if you could show me. Amen."

 Write your prayer here.

Yes! Asking God for wisdom is a wise thing to do.

You Can Ask God To Guide You

"Trust in the Lord with all your heart; do not depend on your own understanding. Seek his will in all you do, and he will show you which path to take."

Proverbs 3:5-6

JOSIAH

I was only 8 years old when I became king. I didn't know how to be a king! But I did know how to pray, so I asked God to guide me.

And God led me to some amazing discoveries! I found the old books that contained all of God's instructions and wise words. It made me sad to know that my people hadn't been following God the way we should.

So I took the old books and shared them with all the people. And together we began to find our way again.

When you're young, it's hard to know exactly where to go and what to do. But that's why prayer is so important. You can talk to God and ask him to show you the way. God promises to guide your steps.

Let's Pray

Ask God to guide you to do the right thing today.

Here's an example:

"Dear God, my friends are choosing to do the wrong thing, and they want me to do it, too. Please help me know how to make the right choice. Amen."

Very good! Do your best to do the right thing today.

Write your prayer here.

You Can Tell God You're Sorry

"But if we confess our sins to him, he is faithful and just to forgive us our sins and to cleanse us from all wickedness."

1 John 1:9

BALAAM

As far as I know, I'm the only guy in the world with a talking donkey. But I'm not the only guy in the world who's made a bad choice.

My donkey has always been faithful and reliable. But one day I was riding him on the way to visit the king of Moab. God didn't want me to go, so he sent an angel to block my path. I didn't see the angel, but my donkey did. My donkey kept stopping, and I started getting mad. I got so angry that I yelled at my donkey and hit him. To my surprise, my donkey yelled back, "Why are you hitting me?"

I had to apologize. I told my donkey I was sorry for hitting him. I told the angel I was sorry for not seeing him. I knew I needed to listen more carefully to what God wanted to tell me.

All of us do the wrong thing from time to time. And when we do the wrong thing, we can hurt our friends. Prayer is a great way to tell God we're sorry for the hurtful things we've done. And you know what? God has promised to forgive us!

63

Let's Pray

Tell God you're sorry about something you've done wrong.

Here's an example:

"God, I lied to my parents yesterday, and I feel terrible about it. I'm sorry. Please forgive me. Amen."

 **Write your prayer here.**

And God says, "You're forgiven!"
Leave those bad things behind.

64

You **CAN** Pray
WITH
Other People

"For where two or three gather together as my followers, I am there among them."

Matthew 18:20

RUTH and NAOMI

When all the men in our family died, all we had left was each other. It was a sad, hard time, but we got through it because we stuck together... and we stuck with God.

We know the importance of being friends. Not only are we friends with each other but we're also friends with God. And since God is our friend, we can talk to God together.

Talking to God isn't something you have to do by yourself. You can join a friend, a family member, or a whole group of friends and pray together. God hears all of you—every word. And God even says that when you pray together with other people, he's right there by your side.

Let's Pray

Pray with a friend or family member.

With a friend, pray together: "God, we pray for our good friend who's been sick at home the past couple of days. Please help her to feel better. Amen."

 Write your prayer here.

Way to team up! Praying together makes you stronger.

YOU CAN THANK GOD FOR ANYTHING

"Devote yourselves to prayer with an alert mind and a thankful heart."

Colossians 4:2

JOB

On one hand, you could say I had a really hard life. I lost all my children and all my money, and I got very, very sick. It would have been easy for me to get mad and blame God for taking away so many wonderful things in my life.

On the other hand, I still had so much to be thankful for—despite all the terrible things that happened to me. Through it all I still knew that God loved me. And no matter how bad things got, I never blamed God when things didn't go my way.

We all have a thousand things we can thank God for—every bite of food we eat, our homes, our beds, our clothes and shoes, our friends and families, and even the things we don't think about much, like running water, sunshine, and sliced bread.

Whenever you're not sure what to pray about, just start thanking God for the good things in your life. You can thank God for anything!

Let's Pray

Thank God for three things.

Here's an example:

"God, thank you for my shoes. I think they're cool, and they're very comfortable. Thank you for a dad who makes me pancakes every Saturday. That always makes me happy! And thank you for my pet dog. She's cuddly and makes me smile a lot. Amen."

 Write your prayer here.

Good work! Keep an eye out for more things you can be thankful for every day.

Your Prayers Make {God} Happy

"The Lord detests the sacrifice of the wicked, but he delights in the prayers of the upright."

Proverbs 15:8

DANIEL

I loved God with all my heart. And no one could stop me from praying. When the king made praying against the law, I still prayed to God morning, noon, and night. Even when the king tossed me into a den with hungry lions, I trusted in God.

I knew something the king didn't know—that God sees everything. God knows exactly what's going on in our lives. Our prayers are never a surprise to God.

Our prayers make God happy!

It's good to know that God *wants* you to talk to him. Anytime, anywhere, about anything. If you want to bring more joy to God's heart, then just talk to him. In fact, talk to God a *lot*!

Let's Pray

Write your prayer here.

Tell God why praying makes you happy.

Here's an example:

"Dear God, I love praying because it makes me feel close to you. I imagine you smiling when I talk to you. That makes me smile, too. Amen."

Put a big smile on your face! Praying always makes you feel better.

You Can Say the Lord's Prayer

"Our Father in heaven, may your name be kept holy. May your Kingdom come soon. May your will be done on earth, as it is in heaven. Give us today the food we need, and forgive us our sins, as we have forgiven those who sin against us. And don't let us yield to temptation, but rescue us from the evil one."

Matthew 6:9-13

JESUS

I know a lot of people aren't sure what to do when they want to pray. They don't want to do it wrong, like the Pharisees who prayed very long prayers and prayed loudly so everyone could hear them.

Your prayer is simply a chat with God. Talking to God is just like talking to a friend. It's not a time to show off, and it isn't hard. When you pray, you can praise God, ask him for what you need, ask him to forgive you and to protect you.

I wanted to show people how easy it is to pray. So I gave them an example. It went like this:

"Our Father in heaven, may your name be kept holy. May your Kingdom come soon. May your will be done on earth, as it is in heaven. Give us today the food we need, and forgive us our sins, as we have forgiven those who sin against us. And don't let us yield to temptation, but rescue us from the evil one."

Isn't that easy? You can pray this prayer, or you can use your own words. Either way, God is pleased that you're talking to him.

Let's Pray

Pray the Lord's Prayer.

"Our Father in heaven, may your name be kept holy. May your Kingdom come soon. May your will be done on earth, as it is in heaven. Give us today the food we need, and forgive us our sins, as we have forgiven those who sin against us. And don't let us yield to temptation, but rescue us from the evil one. Amen."

 Write your prayer here.

*Amen! You can pray the Lord's Prayer
anytime you're not sure what to say.*

YOU CAN PRAY WHEN YOU'RE ANGRY

"But I say, love your enemies!
Pray for those who persecute you!"

Matthew 5:44

JONAH

I didn't like the people who lived in the city of Nineveh. They were awful, nasty people who deserved to be punished. But for some reason, God loved them anyway. God wanted to forgive them. And God wanted me to tell them that.

That made me mad! I refused to do it. In fact, I ran as far away from Nineveh as I could. And then I got into a whole lot of trouble. But three days and nights in the belly of a big fish set me straight.

I went to Nineveh and did what God told me to do. And sure enough, the people there said they were sorry and stopped their wicked ways.

That made me mad, too! They didn't deserve forgiveness! You can be sure I told God how angry I was. Even though I was enraged, God listened to me. God let me tell him how I felt. That didn't mean I was right, but God still listened.

God will always listen to you, too—even when you're upset. If you ever feel mad at a person or a situation—or even God himself—you can tell God about it. And God will hear you.

 # Let's Pray

 Write your prayer here.

Tell God about something that makes you mad.

Here's an example:

"Dear God, I don't like it when people I love fight with each other. It makes me so upset, and I don't like feeling that way. Help me find a way to stay positive. Amen."

Doesn't it feel good to get that off your chest?

79

YOU CAN PRAY WHEN YOU'RE SAD

*"Answer me when I call to you,
O God who declares me innocent.
Free me from my troubles. Have
mercy on me and hear my prayer."*

Psalm 4:1

STEPHEN

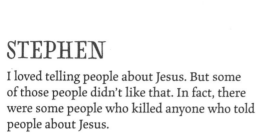

I loved telling people about Jesus. But some of those people didn't like that. In fact, there were some people who killed anyone who told people about Jesus.

The religious leaders who wanted to kill me didn't believe that Jesus was God's Son. They didn't understand that Jesus could live in their hearts. It made me sad that they rejected Jesus—and me.

The best thing for me to do was pray. I talked to God even during my last breath. I asked God to forgive the men who hurt me.

You can always talk to God when you're hurting or going through a hard time. God will always hear you when you're sad, and he promises to comfort you.

Let's Pray

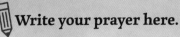 **Write your prayer here.**

Tell God about something that makes you sad.

Here's an example:

"Dear God, I saw a poor person begging on the sidewalk today, and it made me sad. Help me know the best way to give a hand to people who need it. Amen."

It's okay to be sad. Just remember God is always with you.

You Can Pray When You're Confused

"Are any of you suffering hardships? You should pray."

James 5:13a

THOMAS

I loved Jesus. I really did. And when I watched Jesus die, it was the saddest day of my life. I saw them bury his body in a tomb. He was gone.

So when my friends said they'd seen Jesus alive, I just couldn't believe it. Sure, I wanted it to be true. But how could it be?

I was doubtful and confused...which is the perfect time to pray. Whenever we don't understand something, the best place to go is to God. We can always talk to God about why we're confused.

And you know what? He'll hear you. God doesn't mind if you have doubts or questions. So just ask! He loves to hear from you, even if you've got some hard questions.

Let's Pray

Tell God about something that makes you confused.

Here's an example:

"God, sometimes I have a hard time believing in you. Help me to have stronger faith in you. Amen."

Now take a deep breath. Feel good knowing God loves you.

 Write your prayer here.

85

You Can Pray when You're Happy

"Are any of you happy?
You should sing praises."

James 5:13b

MARY

When God told me that I would be the mother of his Son, I was a little scared. It was the greatest honor a person could ever get, but it was also a huge responsibility.

But being Jesus' mom made me the happiest person in the world! When Jesus was little, I loved hearing his laughter and seeing his sweet, smiling face. It brought me so much joy to raise Jesus every day and watch him grow up.

It was easy praying to God during all those happy times with Jesus. God wants us to have joy, and lots of it. And God loves to hear us tell him how happy we are!

Anytime you've got a smile on your face, be sure to tell God what makes you so happy. And don't forget to thank God for bringing those joyful things into your life.

Let's Pray

Tell God about something that makes you happy.

Here's an example:

"God, I just love puppies and kittens! Aren't they the cutest? Thank you for puppies and kittens! Amen."

 Write your prayer here.

Yay, yay, yay! Happy is the way to go!

YOU *CAN* PRAY *for* OTHER PEOPLE

"I urge you, first of all, to pray for all people. Ask God to help them; intercede on their behalf, and give thanks for them."

1 Timothy 2:1

PETER

Jesus told us there are two things we can do that are more important than anything else. He said we need to love God and love people.

Well, I spent my whole life doing just that! I traveled far and wide to tell people about Jesus, and all along the way I looked for people I could help. Sometimes I healed them, and sometimes we just talked. But I always prayed *and* helped them whenever I could.

God loves it when we pray for people. God also loves it when we pray and *do* something for people. Whenever we can lend a hand or do something kind, that's the best way to put our prayers into action.

Let's Pray

Pray for someone you know.

Here's an example:

"Dear God, my grandma is really sick right now. Please help her feel better. Amen."

 Write your prayer here.

Excellent prayer! Praying for others is always a good thing.

YOU'LL ALSO LOVE...

FREE Bible App

Experience the Bible in a more personal way with the free *Friends With God* app.

Available on the App Store — Android App on Google play

Friends With God Story Bible

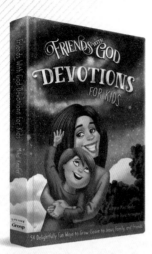

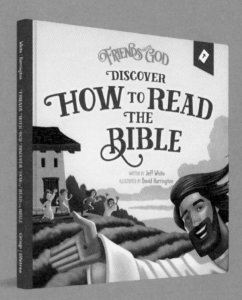

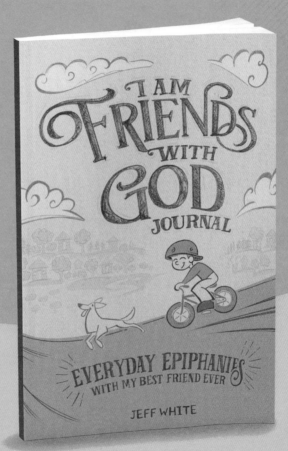

I Am Friends With God Journal

Friends With God Activity Book

"Always pray and never give up."

Luke 18:1